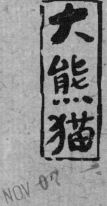

The author, illustrator, and publisher would like to thank Heather Angel, MSc, for her advice and guidance in the preparation of this book.

Text copyright © 2007 by Nick Dowson
Illustrations copyright © 2007 by Yu Rong

First U.S. edition 2007

Library of Congress
Cataloging-in-Publication Data
is available.

Library of Congress Catalog Card Number pending

ISBN 978-0-7636-3146-8

2 4 6 8 10 9 7 5 3 1

Printed in Singapore

This book was typeset in Green.
The illustrations were done in watercolor.

Candlewick Press
2067 Massachusetts Avenue
Cambridge, Massachusetts 02140

visit us at www.candlewick.com

For my mum
N. D.

In memory
of my beloved
father
Y. R.

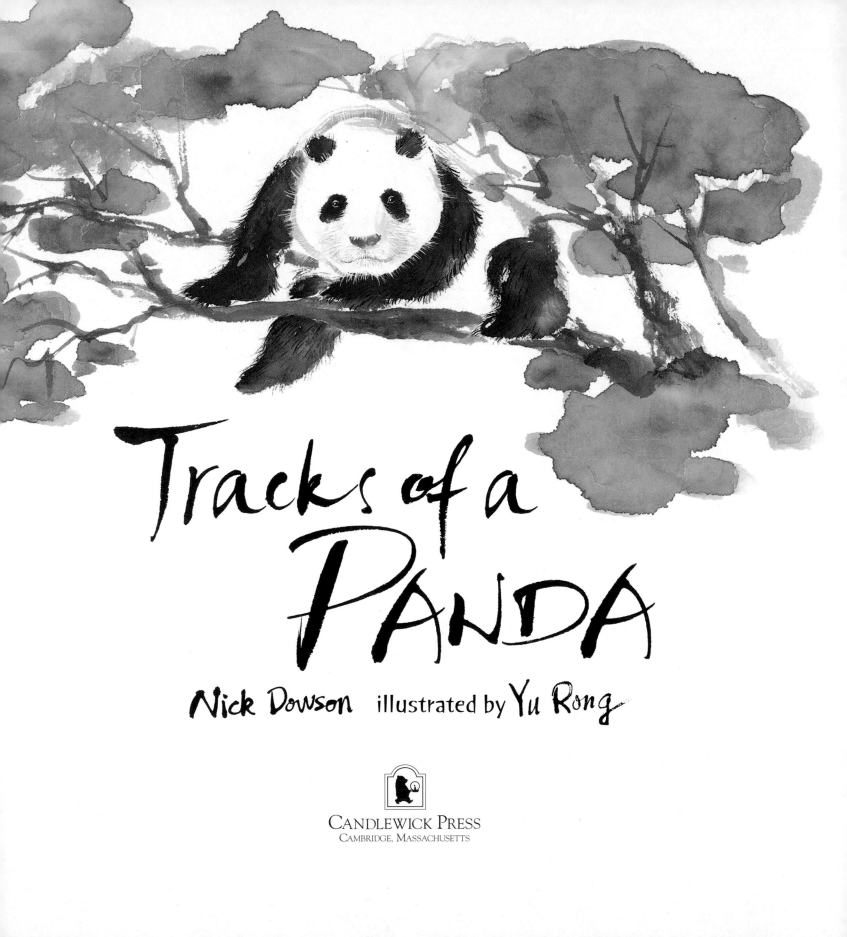

Tracks of a PANDA

Nick Dowson   illustrated by Yu Rong

CANDLEWICK PRESS
CAMBRIDGE, MASSACHUSETTS

*H*igh on a
mist-wrapped mountain,
cradled in a leafy nest,
Panda holds her newborn cub
gently in her giant paw.

Small as a pinecone,
pink as a blob of
wriggling sunset,
he sinks, squawking, into
his mother's fur
until her warm milk
fills his mouth.

Panda cubs
are born blind
and almost
furless.
They are
900 times
smaller than
their mothers.

For days Panda stays with her cub
in their hollow tree den.
But the need to feed herself
grows stronger, and
one bright August morning
she leaves him and
follows her old tracks
to the patch of
bamboo grass where she eats.

There are many
different kinds
of bamboo,
but pandas
usually choose
to eat only
a few kinds.

Pandas have very big back teeth to help them crush tough bamboo stems.

She rolls on her back in
a soft bed of ferns and grabs a
handful of bamboo.
Slowly her big black nose wrinkles:
these leaves smell good
and she is very hungry.
Before she goes back to cuddle
and suckle her cub,
Panda strips
ten stems bare.

For seven weeks the cub's eyes stay shut.
He feeds and sleeps, cries and gurgles.
As he grows, around his ears and eyes,
across his legs, and like a road of
hairy ink on his back,
some of his fur
darkens, like his
mom's, into black.

One fall day, he crawls up Panda's chest
onto her neck. Something cold and wet
tickles his nose, and his eyes open for the
first time — onto a world of falling snow.

It takes four
years for panda
cubs to be as big
as their mothers.

The cub grows fast through winter.

He still climbs and plays on his mother, but now he also takes

his first steps along the mountain tracks.

But Panda has not eaten well for weeks.
Her bamboo patch is dying. Now that her cub is
six months old and strong enough to travel,
she knows they must find a new home .

Pandas' black and
white fur is good
camouflage in winter.

Below her old territory,
the path is steep.
Weak with hunger,
Panda stumbles
and bumps her cub into
a deep drift of snow.

She goes to him and
smells an unexpected
buried meal there.
Snow flies as she scrapes.
This deer meat is old
but will give her strength.

Pandas almost always
eat bamboo, but they
sometimes eat other
things — such as
insects, fish, or meat.

After eating, Panda
suckles her sleepy cub,
then, thirsty, drinks
from a stream.

A shadow slips through
the trees. Closer it comes,
its long tongue lolling.

Panda lifts her big
dripping head.
Like knives, her long
claws slash the air,
and the wild dog growls
and slinks away.

When they
need to defend
their cubs,
mother pandas
are very fierce.

With danger in the forest,
Panda needs a safe
place to sleep:
in a tree.

She hugs the fir's frosty
trunk with both arms, and
her strong claws and
furry feet grip the bark.
Her cub clings to her
shoulder as they clamber
toward the clouds;
then he leaves
her and scrambles
to his own high perch.

Like other bears,
pandas are very
good climbers.

21

When she wakes, Panda suckles her cub but
still needs food for herself. They move on.

Soon she sees a new mountain rising,
with bamboo on its slopes.
Cold water laps at her tired feet,
and she walks into a
stream's dark pool.

To move from
place to place
in the mountains,
pandas need to
be able to swim.

Her paws touch bottom all the way, but in the middle
the cub has to swim. He kicks hard with his feet,
and his paws turn to paddles as he pushes the
water behind him.

Pandas have five "fingers," plus a sixth one, more like a thumb, that helps them hold bamboo.

This new territory
has plenty of food.
Panda won't go hungry now.
Her cub, too,
begins to eat bamboo.
He grips a stem and,
copying his mother,
curls his sticky tongue
around the leaves.

Spring brings warm rain, and juicy
new shoots of bamboo poke up.
One day, mother and cub are
feeding when they hear axes thud
and branches crash nearby.
Panda stops chewing.
Villagers are chopping firewood.
If they move up the mountain,
she and her cub cannot stay.
Slowly she climbs up a deer path,
her cub close behind. . . .

Mother pandas
will not share
territory with
other pandas
or people.

Clouds curl around their tracks as they go.

Their hunt for a new home is beginning again.

Index

Look up the pages to find out
about all these panda things.
Don't forget to look at both kinds
of words — **this kind**
and this kind.

About the author

Nick Dowson is a teacher and writer. He loves wild places and the animals that live there. "Mountains are where I like to be the most," he says, "just like the giant panda."

About the illustrator

Yu Rong studied Chinese art in Nanjing before moving to London, where she received a master's degree from the Royal College of Art. "I've never seen a wild panda," she says, "but I know the mountain country where they like to live."

About pandas

Giant pandas live only in a few high mountain forests in southwest China. Because female pandas raise just one cub at a time, panda numbers are slow to grow. It does not help that poachers still hunt them and loggers threaten their habitat. Where special reserves are set up to protect them, pandas do well. Even so, their future survival is at risk: there are only about 2,500 wild giant pandas left.